1 MONTH OF
FREE
READING

at

www.ForgottenBooks.com

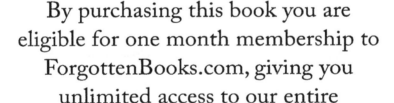

By purchasing this book you are eligible for one month membership to ForgottenBooks.com, giving you unlimited access to our entire collection of over 1,000,000 titles via our web site and mobile apps.

To claim your free month visit:
www.forgottenbooks.com/free797308

ISBN 978-0-483-97339-8
PIBN 10797308

REMINISCENCES

OF THE

LATE REV. WILLIAM T. SPROLE, D. D.

BY ENOCH L. FANCHER. LL.D.

RITCHIE & HÜLL,
Journal Printing House and Book-Bindery,
Newburgh, N. Y.

REMINISCENCES

OF THE

LATE WILLIAM T. SPROLE, D. D.,

BY ENOCH L. FANCHER, LL.D.

I.

IN the *Detroit Evening News*, of Monday, June 11, 1883, appeared the following:

"Rev. Dr. William T. Sprole died at his home, 72 Miami Avenue, late Saturday evening, closing a career of active ministerial work, extending over nearly half a century. Dr. Sprole was born at Baltimore in 1809. He was educated at Princeton Theological Seminary, and after graduation assumed charges at Philadelphia and Carlisle, Pa., successively. In 1842 he accepted a call to the First Presbyterian Church at Washington, where he remained five years, and during his residence there also discharged the duties of chaplain in the House of Representatives. In 1847 he was appointed Professor of Ethics and Law in the West Point Military Academy. Ten years later he resigned his

professorship, having received a call from the First Presbyterian
Church at Newburgh. In 1874 he came to Detroit to accept the
pastorate of the Second Congregational Church, to which he had
been called, succeeding the Rev. Mr. Freeman. He resigned this
charge in 1877, and has since been engaged in general evangelical
work and acting as a supply pastor up to his last fatal illness.
Dr. Sprole was a typical old school gentleman, with much of the
military spirit in his bearing, and he possessed oratorical abilities
of a high order. He was honored with the degree of D. D. by
several different colleges. Besides his wife, four children survive
him, Samuel M. Sprole, of Brooklyn, N. Y.; Capt. Henry W.
Sprole, of the Eighth United States Cavalry, stationed at San
Antonio, Texas; Mrs. Dr. Dunster, of Ann Arbor, and Mrs.
Eastman, of Minneapolis. The funeral takes place from the
First Presbyterian Church to-morrow at 2 P. M., and the remains
will be taken to Indianapolis for burial."

The lady referred to as his wife, in the above notice, was the
second wife of Doctor Sprole. His first wife, the mother of his
children, died, a number of years ago, while on a visit to her
daughter in the city of New York.

I propose a brief record of some reminiscences of Dr.
Sprole, who, for years, was my intimate friend. A good life
awakens memories like a charming melody. The refrain returns
to touch the sensibilities long after it is spent. Its well-remem-
bered parts are recalled and the perception of their excellence
is revived. When we have long shared the counsel and the
companionship of a beloved friend, who has now gone, we
retrospect every familiar scene of his life with a former delight.

From his example we are encouraged to imitate his virtues, and to follow in his pathways.

It seems beneficial to dwell on the characteristics of the great and good; to enter into their experiences, and to study their habits. A review of their traits of character tends to stimulate our own endeavors, and lures us to copy after them. Above that of any other, the life of a faithful Christian minister portrays phases of incident and interest, but its history deepens into pathos, as we stand, in contemplation, near his new-made grave. The memory of such, though blessed, is mingled with regret. That of the subject of this sketch is fresh and fragrant; yet the undertone of sadness is very deep as one attempts to write of him. He had such vigorous life; such uninterrupted health; such strength of constitution, such manly form, and such physical endurance,—all which gave so much promise of an unusually lengthened life, that it is sad to think of him now as dead, and of his earthly companionship and friendship as gone forever.

He was endowed with a healthful and robust mind, so cultivated as to be ever strong to perceive and cherish the right, and ever ready the wrong to discover and resist. His talents were employed for much benefit to others during a long and active life. He had a felicitous power to aid and cheer any who needed encouragement, and there was such friendliness in his help, that the high and the humble were alike grateful to him. There was force in his words adequate to contend against veteran opposers of the truth, and there was at the same time exhibited such manifest interest in their welfare that a friendly persuasion went along with a convincing argument. He knew, and practiced, the art of being apparently one with the humble and lowly. He cared for them as if he had a special mission in their behalf.

In controversy, forced upon him but never sought, his sword was thoroughly sharp, his powder ever dry, and his confidence of triumph in a righteous cause, well sustained. He powerfully reasoned of righteousness, temperance, and a judgment to come. That he never yielded to impatience under provocation, need not be denied; but his wonderful reserve of self-reliant power, made him, in any emergency, complete master of the situation. His position was maintained with heroic confidence.

I first met Dr. Sprole when he had recently left the chaplaincy and a professorship at West Point, and had accepted a call from the First Presbyterian Church at Newburgh, N. Y., to become its pastor. My summer home at "Elfwood," was about three miles distant; we often met, and our opening acquaintance speedily ripened into the warmest friendship. In physical appearance he was then a model of manly strength. His carriage was stately and dignified; his voice clear and musical; his eye loving and penetrating; his conversation fluent and instructive, and his movements and gestures wore the charm of surpassing grace and self-composure. Nature in unmistakable characters had stamped him with her signet of manliness.

I went to Newburgh each Sabbath during summer to hear him preach. He began his ministry to the congregation there in the old church where the late Dr. Johnston had been for half a century the pastor. The edifice was immediately crowded. Even the gallery pews were in full demand. I was forced to go there myself, and occupied sittings immediately behind the front gallery pew, in which was constantly seated the Rev. Dr. Potts, when he was spending his vacation at Newburgh. He appeared to be one of the most entranced listeners of the audience. It was interesting to watch the play of subdued emotion on the faces of those who crowded that edifice. During the sermon, a solemn silence was kept, and every eye was turned on the preacher. At passages of his discourse, delivered in the ringing cadences of his strong and well-modulated voice, the hearers would evince a rapt attention, and sometimes bend toward the speaker like a field of grain. The more lofty the theme, the more perfectly it was touched under the hand of its master. A lasting perfume seemed to arise from his eloquent discourses, embalming their influence in the 'heart long after their delivery in that old, well-filled church, with its crowded galleries.

The edifice soon became too small to accommodate the con-

gregation to whom he ministered. It was consequently proposed that a larger structure should be erected; but there were
many who long had worshipped in the old church, to whom
the straight-backs of the painted pews, and the familiar old-style
pulpit, seemed sacred. Their fathers had worshipped there;
they and their children had been baptised and received into
communion there; it was there that the last look at the
forms of dear departed ones had been taken; they thought
of the tears shed at the chancel of that old church, and could
careless hands tear it down? It was little less, in their esti-
mation, than sacrilege! Yet the necessity of larger accommo-
dations was so apparent, that a majority of the congregation
resolved upon the undertaking. Lots were secured at the
corner of Grand and South Streets, and on which a new
stone edifice was erected, leaving the old one to stand. For
a time some portion of the remaining congregation continued
to worship in the old wooden edifice; but they, too, soon
yielded to the pressure of events. It was taken down and a
new one of brick arose in its place.

In the edifice newly erected by the trustees of Dr. Sprole's
congregation, he officiated for about sixteen years. I usually
attended service there every Sabbath morning in summer.
His congregation rapidly increased, and was as select as any
in the city. His sermons there were eloquent expositions of
sacred truths—always sound and orthodox.

There was a mutual understanding between us that he was to visit "Elfwood," on Monday. Then, in the confidence and intimacy of social converse, I ever found him overflowing with information, cordiality and friendship. His company was most enjoyable. He had been in contact with many public men, both of the Church and the State, and, touching them, his reminiscences and anecdotes were many and entertaining. His conversation was remarkable for pungent wit, and terse, almost epigramatic, language. Solid learning, general reading, retentive memory, and mental activity, enabled him readily to evoke from the stores of his knowledge and observation, abundant matter of amusement and instruction. A pleasant anecdote, or a jocose remark, was delivered with the same calm voice as when discoursing on more sober themes; but none failed to notice the twinkle of his eyes as he thus spoke, or the compression of his lips as they pent up the struggling smile. He loved to talk, and bore a prominent share in the conversation, though he rarely suggested the topic on which it was to turn, but politely left that to others. Yet he readily took up whatever was suggested by those around, and then drew rich treasures of thought and information from the mine they had unconsciously opened. His tone and manner when in the social circle were touched with a quiet and grave humor, promoting, not infrequently, a sort of subdued jocularity, that gave much zest and effect to his utterances;

but he knew well when and where to lay aside the lighter and adopt the graver language and manner.

He honored me with occasional visits at my home in New York; and then as we were alone at evening, it was generally long past the hour of the "keystone of night's black arch" before we retired. His conversation breathed the purity of chastened thought and agreeable familiarity, when thus unrestrained. That we loved each other's society I fondly knew. Refinement, originality, courteousness, instructive conversation, and affectionate regard, added to the value of so familiar and trusted a friend. He consented to receive my .reciprocal expressions of regard, and would recognize them in a voice tremulous with emotion. One Saturday as he came to my residence, I requested that he allow me to mention his presence in the city, to my pastor, the Rev. Dr. McClintock, whom I knew at the time to be unwell and in need of pulpit assistance for the next day. The pastor of St. Paul's had formed the acquaintance of Dr. Sprole at Carlisle, Pa., and very gladly at once solicited him to preach in the morning. Dr. Sprole did so, and was at his best, though in a Methodist pulpit. He delivered, without notes, one of the grandest of sermons. The congregation, while listening, supposed he was some distinguished Methodist preacher. For the evening, Dr. McC. had procured a supply from a preacher somewhat sensational in style. What a contrast there was between the morning and the evening discourse! Dr. Sprole that evening sat with me in my pew, and the Rev. Dr. Forsyth was also there. As these two scholarly and popular preachers were walking in the aisle side by side toward the door of the church, at the conclusion of the evening service, I overheard Dr. Sprole quietly remark to Dr. Forsyth,— "John! you and I don't know how to preach! that's the man!" The humor and irony of the remark befitted the occasion. I said to him, "Doctor, is that some of 'the hub?'" "No," he returned, "It's the periphery!"

He left no effort untried to gain over to a religious life non-professors who came within the sphere of his influence. Among such was a distinguished citizen of Newburgh. That gentleman, under Dr. Sprole's ministry, became, late in life, a devout member of his church, and died so, much respected and beloved. But while the struggle against conviction of duty and a liking for an occasional glass was going on, I met him one warm evening at a crowded party. Seeing him indulging in a glass of champagne, I remarked to him, "I thought Dr. Sprole had induced you to sign the temperance pledge." "Yes," he replied, "but this is a very drouthy time, and *all signs* fail in a drouth!" His well-intended purpose, however, soon triumphed, and he became a worthy member of the church, and strictly temperate in his habits.

For one entire summer, whatever was the topic of discourse, the Doctor seldom omitted some reference to the subject of temperance. He thought there was occasion for that peculiarity and earnestness in the state of society at the time. He inveighed against "tippling," and the use of intoxicating stimulants, with constant zeal. In one of his visits at "Elfwood," he complained of slight indisposition. I suggested a spoonful of old brandy in some water. He demurred, and said he had nothing of the kind in his house, and would not on any account purchase the stuff. I had some long-stored brandy, and, as he was leaving, placed a bottle of it on the seat of his buggy. He put his hand on it so carelessly, with such doubtful dislike to accept it that I said, "Doctor, you'll break that bottle before you reach home! don't do it; it's good for medicine and that bottle is valuable and choice."

He met me the next morning with a smile, in the street at Newburgh, and said, "You are a true prophet. I did break that bottle, and the contents are lost." He had placed it at one side of the carriage-house, and hung the harness on a nail over it; the nail gave way, and the fall of the harness broke the bottle. "But," said he, "the *aroma* was very fine!" So far as I know, that was his first and last attempt at transporting a bottle of brandy to the parsonage.

He was a favorite of my gardener, and saluted him with

courtly formality as if an equal. One day, the Attorney-General of the United States came from West Point, and while calling on Dr. Sprole remarked that his wife was ill at the Point, and he had vainly looked for some fruit for her. The Doctor said, "I have a friend near this place, and will drive down there with you; perhaps he has some peaches." I was absent when they arrived, but the Doctor and the Attorney-General entered my garden, and, meeting the gardener, the Doctor said: "Mr. William! permit me to introduce the Attorney-General of the United States!" William was petrified; but stammered, "God bless you, Mr. Attorney-General!—look at the peaches!" Of course, he obtained some of them to take to his wife, as well as some for his own enjoyment. I was more than compensated for the early "rare-ripes" by the Doctor's relation of the visit, and by the kind and cordial remembrances left for me by the distinguished official.

Dr. Sprole had a noble spirit of commisseration for the misguided and the unhappy. On one of his visits to me, in New York, he talked of the condition of a young man then under sentence of death for the murder of a police officer. The day of execution was appointed for the ensuing Friday. As he spoke of the supposed agony of the mother, he noticed my own want of composure. I explained to him the cause. I was then one of the Justices of the Supreme

Court, and on that very day I had been listening to the importunate argument of counsel for a writ of error and stay of execution in the case of the young man to whom the Doctor had referred. I saw no proper ground for granting the application, and knew, if I did not, the execution would take place in less than a week. Terrible as is the death penalty, it seemed to me proper in that case it should not be stayed, there being but slight ground of an appeal; and I stated to the Doctor my conclusion. He did not oppose me in the matter; but the great deep of his undisguised sorrow seemed to be stirred. How he sympathized with the disconsolate relatives of the miserable young man, though he knew them not, and how gladly, were it proper, would he have averted his impending doom! I think that sleepless and painful hours were passed that night by at least two persons who were not related to, or acquainted with, the convict. For myself, it was one of the most trying occasions of my life; but duty called me to the task, and I wrote an opinion adverse to the stay.

I saw Dr. Sprole on another occasion, when he was more agitated, and was even broken down with grief. Late at night I was awakened from sleep by the ringing of my door bell. Raising the window, I called to know who was there, and at once recognized his answering voice sobbing and crying. "My dear wife is dying," said he, "will you come?" I accompanied him to his daughter's residence, and gazed for some time at the death scene. Mrs. Sprole was unconscious, and had been from her first and recent sudden attack. Death, from apoplexy, soon occurred; and while I promised to go for the undertaker, he prepared to go to Newburgh to arrange for the solemn ceremony of the funeral.

He who had so often sympathized with others in bereavement, and had exhorted them to composure and resignation, was now himself sadly in need of a sympathetic voice to assuage his sorrow and to calm his agitation.

Did he remember me for then attempting such a ministry of friendship, that in after years, in a similar sorrow of my own, he poured forth such consoling utterances and spoke such healing words, that I shall never forget them? I supposed he was in Detroit when the sad visitation came to my home, and I penned a telegram to him which I was carrying to Newburgh to be forwarded, when, to my surprise, I saw him coming toward me in Colden Street. As we met I handed to him the telegram, requesting his presence at the funeral of my wife. It was the first he had learned of her decease. We were both so much overcome, that few words then passed. But, at the funeral, his address was most tender, appropriate, and impressive. "I feel," said he, as he began, "that my place is among the mourners." "Here," said he, in his prayer, at the grave, "may this dear body rest, un-

disturbed by the fury of the elements or the violence of
the wicked, till Christ shall bid it rise." He had been her
beloved pastor and much attached friend, and his kind
words, evoked by her lamented departure, are still. ringing
in my memory.

It is sad to think that he, himself, has gone, and I shall
hear his familiar voice no more. Yet, so it is.

> " There is dust upon his brow,
>   And coldness in that kindly heart,
>   That ne'er was cold till now."

Had he lived longer, and could our intercourse have been
continued, how much I should have learned from the wisdom
of his ripest years! As it lengthened, more and more I
valued his friendship. He had so much wit for the social,
and so much wisdom for the serious, hour. When I had
been with him there was a feeling that something had been
added to my life. I had been breathing a purer moral and
religious air. His words would touch the heart with tender-
ness and inspire a reverence for every sacred theme on
which . he dilated. Walking with him along life's winding
shores, was like looking into the calm of both blue depths—
the great ocean beneath and the infinite sky above. He ever
saw the morning light that would dawn after the changes of
this oft-darkened world, and that dawn was illumined with
eternal glory.

As one has said, there is an unquenchable thirst of the soul that is a strong proof of its divine nature; a thirst not to be allayed with the turbid waters of any earthly good, nor of all earthly enjoyments taken together. It thirsts after a good, invisible, immaterial, and immortal.

It was the frequent practice of Dr. Sprole to discourse upon such high and absorbing themes; and then, cold was the heart that did not throb beneath his utterances. There was a peculiar charm in his manner, and a singular force in his speech.

I have not opportunity to consider the work which he accomplished in his ministry of fifty years, nor to allude to the varied subjects he discussed in his well prepared sermons, though I have been favored with the notes of several of his discourses. They show with what care, judgment, and mastery of the subjects, he was accustomed to write; but for them the limits of a sketch have no room. Nor could the cold reproduction of his written thoughts be made to exhibit the magnetism of personal presence and manner, nor the adaptation to the special occasions when they were delivered. To appreciate his abilities as a preacher, it were necessary both to see and to hear him. That countenance so expressive; that voice so clear; that tone so modulated; that eye so beaming; that gesture so appropriate; that flash o'er the features, and that following peal of such force and energy that

it seemed launched from some Olympian throne of thought:
these were elements of his preaching. Only thus could one
look through the eloquent style, to perceive the golden threads
that glittered in the discourse. It is through the crystal
waters of the deep sea that pearls appear distinct, and large,
and near; and so the arts of expression hold up to clearer
view the truths that had otherwise appeared but dim.

There should be added, of course, in any sketch of Dr.
Sprole, the element of an upright, faithful, and consistent life.
His character was that of a true Christian. It had the
charm which belongs to a noble and beautiful nature. He
was possessed of a pleasing affability, free from all affecta-
tion, and, in harmony with those traits, he combined a dignity
of deportment that showed his self-command and his cultured
manner. But all he had—time, culture, eloquence, manner,
and influence, he consecrated to the great work of a Christian
minister with untiring zeal. He who was so lately speaking
to us here, that his voice seems yet to be heard, is now beyond
the sun. I reverently pause, to drop the friendly tear and
to record a loving tribute to his memory.

> "He bore his great commission in his look,
> And preached the Gospel rather than the law."

II.

RECOLLECTIONS BY REV. JOHN FORSYTH, D. D.

MY DEAR JUDGE FANCHER: When we met at the New Windsor Centennial you told me that it was proposed to publish a memorial of our old and dear friend, the late Dr. Sprole, more permanent than a simple funeral sermon, and you asked me to give my recollections of him. Since then I am delighted to learn that the task of preparing the Memoir of him has been placed in your hands. Certainly no one is better fitted than yourself to render a proper tribute to his memory, as your close friendship with him for many years must have enabled you to appreciate his qualities as a man, as a Christian, and a pastor and preacher. For myself I can hardly hope to add anything of moment to what has been so well said in regard to him by the Rev. Mr. Sutherland at Indianapolis, and more recently by the Rev. Mr. Gardiner, a former pastor of the Presbyterian Church, of Cold Spring, in the *New York Evangelist*. Still I most heartily join with them in doing honor to his memory by bringing my chaplet to lay upon his grave.

I well remember my first introduction to Dr. Sprole by his and my dear old friend, the Rev. Dr. John Chambers, for many years the eminently successful pastor of an Independent church in Philadelphia. It was in the old Ranstead Court Church during a meeting of the General Assembly of the Presbyterian Church, at the time when the bitter war between the Old and the New School was on the point of culminating in the disruption which split that Church into two hostile bands, which, however, were happily re-united in 1869. I had been just ordained and installed pastor of the Associate Reformed Church (now the Second United Presbyterian Church of that city, of which my dear friend and successor, the Rev. Dr. J. B. Dales is pastor); while Dr. Sprole had been for some three or four years pastor of one of the German Reformed churches, and had already made his mark as a very popular preacher and pastor. Brought up as I was in one of the branches of the Scottish Presbyterian Church, my sympathies then were decidedly Old School. Dr. Sprole's, on the contrary, though then and always Old School in his theology, were with the New School, on account of the larger liberty of theological thought which that school demanded, but more especially on account of its real or supposed zeal for revivals. Born and educated as he was in the Presbyterian Church, he naturally took a deep interest in the contest between these schools; and it was doubtless due to the fact just mentioned, that he was called to succeed Dr. George Duffield in the First Presbyterian Church, of Carlisle; and at a later day to become pastor of the First Presbyterian Church, of Washington. The same year that he was called to Carlisle, I went to Newburgh as pastor of Union Church, and Professor in the Theological Seminary of the A. R. Church.

My intimacy with Dr. Sprole did not really begin until after he came to West Point, as Professor and Chaplain in the Military Academy. It was, perhaps, partly owing to the fact that I had had the offer of the position by President Polk; an honor which I owed to the influence of Dr. Sprole, and my old friend General A. C. Niven, then member of Congress from this district, but which I was compelled to decline, as I had been at the same time elected a Professor in the College of New Jersey, at Princeton. During my collegiate vacation we saw a good deal of each other, and the more thoroughly I came to know, the higher did he rise in my esteem. I can never forget one Sunday that I spent with him at West Point. It was the first Sunday on which he administered the Lord's Supper in the 'Chapel of the Academy. As Dr. Sprole, of course, used on this occasion the Presbyterian ritual, the number of communicants was very small, and it included only one member of the corps of cadets. His address at the table was one of the best I ever have heard. During my connexion with the Military Academy, I often wished that he could have been present on one of our communion Sundays, and at the cadet prayer meeting on a Sunday evening. I am very sure that his heart would have been made glad by the great contrast, and with the evidence of the greatly increased religious influences at work in the corps.

Two of my colleagues in the Military Academy were cadets during Dr. Sprole's incumbency, and they always spoke of him with great respect for his abilities as a preacher and professor. His removal from the Academy by Mr. Jefferson Davis, who was then Secretary of War, considering the way in which it was done, was an outrage of which only such a man as Davis has shown himself to be in other spheres, could have been guilty. It was a contemptible instance of personal revenge. While Davis was a member of the Senate, he had concocted some scheme in reference to the Military Academy to which all the professors were strongly opposed. As Dr. Sprole had many warm friends and old parishioners among the Democratic members of the Senate and the House of Representatives, he was urged to go to Washington and use his influence with them to defeat this scheme of Davis, which he did. When Davis became Secretary of War under President Pierce, he was in a position to "get even" with Dr. Sprole, and he quickly availed himself of it. I have reason to know that all Dr. Sprole's colleagues, even those who would have much preferred to have an Episcopal rather than a Presbyterian Chaplain, were of one mind as to the conduct of Davis in this affair.

I was called back to Newburgh, from Princeton, in 1853, and when in 1856 the First Presbyterian Church became vacant by the death of the venerable Dr. Johnston, it gave me great satisfaction to learn that Dr. Sprole was called to succeed him. The church had been a good deal weakened by division in regard to the choice of a pastor, and a considerable body of its membership had withdrawn to form a new congregation, now known as Calvary Church ; but from the day of Dr. Sprole's settlement, the old congregation entered upon a new career of prosperity, which speedily culminated in the erection of the stately edifice in which they now worship.

Being residents of the same city, and near neighbors, our intimacy became closer than ever, though belonging to different denominations ; and so it continued until my removal to West Point, and his departure from Newburgh about a year later. If he wanted a supply for his pulpit, or help in any special service, he was sure to come to me ; and the memory of the days we have spent together in Christ's work will ever be very precious to me.

That Dr. Sprole was an " able minister of the New Testament " and an eloquent preacher of the Gospel, all who ever were acquainted with him must have been well assured. To those who did not know him, one need only name the important positions he was called to occupy from his entrance on the ministry to its close — in Philadelphia, Carlisle, Washington, West Point, Newburgh, Detroit. Here, in Newburgh, he was a great favorite with our Methodist friends in Trinity and St John's churches. He always appeared in their pulpits without his notes, and his sermons, on these occasions, had a power and an unction more than marked the written ones given to his own people in his own pulpit. The difference was so marked that I often begged him to discard his notes altogether. He was, as you know, a man of very pronounced opinions on certain subjects, *e. g.*, dancing and total abstinence; and he did not hesitate to denounce, with great plainness and vigor, social usages which he deemed inconsistent with the Christian profession. I used to think, and still think, that the influence of his discourses on this class of topics would have been greater than it was if he could have combined in greater measure than he sometimes did, the "suaviter in modo" with the "fortiter in re." Like all other men he had, no doubt, his failings, though in his case they "ever leaned to virtue's side." He was evidently determined to tell men the truth as he understood it, whether they liked it or not; and he will be long remembered in Newburgh as a faithful and eloquent pastor and preacher.

I deeply sympathize with my dear friends, his children, in their great loss. But they have the comfort in thinking that he was so long spared to them; that he now rests from his labors, in the bosom of Jesus; and has bequeathed to them that "good name which is better than great riches."

I am, very truly yours,

JNO. FORSYTH.

NEWBURGH, 20th July, 1883.

III.

REV. WILLIAM T. SPROLE, D. D.

BY REV. A. S. GARDINER.

FROM the *New York Evangelist* of July 5, 1883, the following article is, by permission, copied :

It was with surprise and profound sorrow that the news of
the death of Dr. Sprole came to my ears. I had anticipated for him
a long and vigorous old age, withdrawn as he was from the burdens of the pastorate, and still engaging from time to time in his
life-long work of preaching the Gospel.

It was my pleasure and privilege to know Dr. Sprole as a
personal friend and co-presbyter for over thirty years. Our
acquaintance began in the village of Greenport, N. Y., in the
fall of 1852. At that time I was the minister of the Presbyterian
Church in that village. I remember well how on one Sabbath
morning two gentlemen of noble bearing, followed by two lads,
came up the aisle of the church, and took seats at the right of the
pulpit. I little suspected who they were. But at the close of the
service they stepped forward and introduced themselves, first as
Rev. Mr. Sprole, United States Chaplain at West Point, and then
as Mr. Henry Warner of Constitution Island, on the Hudson.
The lads were the sons of Prof. Sprole. Prof. Sprole said to me
aside that Mr. Warner was the father of the author of the
"Wide, Wide World." To form the acquaintance of two such
gentlemen, was of course a great pleasure to me.

At my urgent request, Prof. Sprole consented to preach in the afternoon. The sermon I shall never forget. The text was the words "For as Moses lifted up the serpent in the wilderness," etc. Its influence is upon me as I write. The illustrations were most original and affecting. And not unfrequently have I employed, in my discourses upon the same text, and with, I may add, unusual effect, the leading thoughts presented on that occasion.

The strong air of the coast was injurious to my health, and the following May I accepted a call to the Presbyterian Church of Cold Spring, on the Hudson, in the heart of the Highlands. This brought me into the near neighborhood of West Point, and therefore of my friends, Prof. Sprole and Mr. Warner. When Dr. Johnston, of Newburgh, was invited to moderate my call, he first consulted with Prof. Sprole, who kindly advised him to proceed. During a pastorate of twelve years at Cold Spring, I had frequent intercourse with Prof. Sprole and his family. We occasionally exchanged pulpit services, as well as family visits. His home was a large stone building. It stood not far from the parade ground, and commanded a fine view of the river. His family at that time consisted of himself, his wife, two daughters, and three sons. A more delightful home circle is rarely found. It was a privilege to enter it. The wife and mother was a woman of affability and dignity combined. Grace marked the daughters, and manliness the sons.

Prof. Sprole was nominated for the Chaplaincy at West Point by President Polk. And he would, no doubt, have continued at that post until retired under the regulations, had it not been for the unfriendly course pursued by Jefferson Davis, then Secretary of War.

The removal took place amid the complications connected with the opening of the Rebellion. It was, no doubt, the outcome of the course which disloyal politicians had resolved to pursue as necessary to carry out more effectually their schemes for the dismemberment of the Republic. The removal was not only unscrupulous, but sudden. It involved Dr. Sprole and his family in serious perplexity. In about a week from the time of the Doctor's interview at Washington with Jefferson Davis, who told him that he should not be hurried from his post, the household goods of the Doctor's successor were at the gate. This course on the part of Mr. Davis met with unqualified condemnation from some of the leading men at the Capitol. General Cass and Robert J. Walker expressed their disapproval and regret, and with others urged the revocation of the order; but in vain. So this act took its place among many others, which distinguished and disgraced the closing period of secession authority at Washington.

But Dr. Sprole, though annoyed and embarrassed by these summary proceedings, was soon invited to other fields of labor. After careful deliberation, he accepted a call to the First Presbyterian Church of Newburgh, N. Y. In place of the edifice where the congregation had previously worshipped, a very large, substantial, and imposing structure was erected, and in this the Doctor preached for many years.

After the resignation of his charge at Newburgh, he spent some time at the West, and at length accepted a call to a large and promising church at Detroit, where he established a home, and where he resided at the time of his death. Accepting a charge at Detroit brought him within easy distance of his elder daughter, wife of one of the Professors of the Medical College at Ann Arbor. It was my privilege to visit him in his new home. I was much gratified to find him surrounded with all the conveniences which makes home attractive. The Doctor had contracted a second marriage. His former wife, of whom I have spoken, had died some years before. The scene, of course, had changed. I had known him when his children were about him; now they were gone. I had known him in the meridian of his strength and usefulness, amid scenes of great interest in both Church and

State; now the excitements of the past were over. Changes such as these deeply affect the heart. It requires no little effort for the mariner long tossed upon tempestuous seas, and accustomed through many years to all the employments and perils of the deep, to content himself with the quiet scenes of life on land. Nor is it less difficult for the soldier inured to the fatigues of marches, and to the fierce encounters of battlefields, to lay aside the accoutrements of war, and to walk the paths of peace, which even his own valor may have helped to win. The thought of complete retirement from the work of the ministry was equally distasteful to our brother. Not that he craved any further prominent place: on the contrary, he wished to spend the remainder of his strength and years in some retired but useful field, where he might bestow the fruits of his long and rich experience in the ministry of the Word. Nothing could more effectually than this relieve the pain incident to the changes which our brother was called to meet. And so it was granted him, after his resignation of the charge at Detroit, to preach on, Providence opening the way, until the Gospel trumpet which he had blown so long, and with no uncertain sound, fell from a nerveless grasp, and the Christian soldier rested from his work.

For those who knew Dr. Sprole, and heard him preach, it is not necessary for me to write. But for others I may say that he was one of the most agreeable preachers that it has ever been my good fortune to hear; and it has been my habit from youth up to wait on the ministry of prominent and acceptable men in country and city alike, and there are but few men of note in this country whom I have not heard. There was a peculiar sweetness, as well as vigor, in what he said. Preaching either with or without notes, his words fell in due order, and were noticeable for elegance, precision, and perspicuity. I recall his preaching with peculiar pleasure. It was sometimes so tender that my eyes were often filled with tears. I shall never forget the sermon to which

I have already referred, nor another preached one Sabbath afternoon at his church in Newburgh. His theme was "The woman
that was a sinner, and who came into the house of Simon the
leper when the Saviour was his guest." The subject was just in
the line of the speaker's genius and sympathies and vivid imagin-
ation, and he brought out the truths involved with great effect.
The audience on that occasion was not large, but I noticed Judge
Betts of the United States Court for the Southern District of New
York, present, and there was not a more attentive listener in all
the assembly.

Dr. Sprole's fine personal presence lent interest to him as a
speaker. He stood full six feet high. He had a military bearing
in all his movements. The expression of his countenance while
indicating firmness was full of sweetness. He was in all
appearances such a speaker as an audience would love to look at
as well as hear. His complexion was a rare mingling of red and
white. His eye was piercing, and there was often a twinkle about
it indicative of humor. His voice was clear and his utterance
distinct. His tones in speech were varied. There was no
monotony. And all combined to make him a captivating pulpit
orator.

In the social circle he always found a welcome. His familiarity
with the different spheres of social life made him at home in all.
With tender word and gentle step he would enter the homes of
the poor, and with the same spirit he visited the homes of the
affluent.

In his intercourse there might be perceived at times a vein of
satire, but it was of the facetious and discriminating kind. On
one occasion when as chaplain he invited me to exchange pulpits
with him, he added, "I want you to understand that I never in-
vite anybody to preach for me that I think smarter than myself."
But I had no discussion to hold, but felt gratified with the kind
attention of my friend, several years my senior, inviting me a

young man to speak even now and then to the cadets and officers
to whom it was his special duty to preach.·

He was kindly considerate of young men, and especially of
young ministers. He often referred to the sermon which I
preached the Sabbath morning when he and his friends attended
my church in Greenport. The subject of it was "Sabbath
schools." Occasionally he would cross the ferry on the Sabbath
and attend service as a hearer at my church in the afternoon. On
one occasion I preached a sermon which deeply moved the feelings of his sympathetic heart. As we left the sanctuary, he said
to me, " Well, brother, it won't do for you and me to sit under
one another's preaching."

In the Presbytery his counsel was sought by his brethren, and
his judgment was regarded. He was always a genial and attentive
member.

In the course of his ministry he enjoyed many honors not
accorded to his brethren. He preached in Washington, with
Senators, Representatives, and the President's family among his
hearers. He acted as chaplain in Congress, and at West Point
he was brought into the society of distinguished persons from
our own country, and from abroad, who visited the Military
Academy.

But with all these honors were mingled afflictions. The sudden
close of his work at West Point was followed not long after with
a much more serious trial. When the war for the Union began,
his eldest son, William, was a young man in business in New
York. He had for some time been a member of the "Seventh
Regiment," and with that regiment he took his departure for
Washington and the front. While stationed on Arlington Heights
he contracted bilious or typhoid fever. He returned to his home,
but returned to die. After a brief illness, he was numbered with
the nation's martyrs. It was a terrible blow to the whole loving
household, but especially to the bereaved father and mother.

How often had I, as a guest beneath the parental roof, heard the father pray for the beloved son, then a stripling amid the temptations of a great city. But now the solicitude was over. But it had given place in the father's and mother's hearts to the cry of the desolate David, "Would God I had died for thee, my son, my son!"

But the mother and son were not to be long separated. She was a woman of deep sensibility, of quick perceptions, of excellent judgment. She lived to see the emptiness of so-called human friendships, of worldly honors, and she turned with satiety away. After a little while she followed her beloved boy to the grave. Nay, she followed him to glory, for he died as he had lived—a Christian. And then and there, under friendlier skies, began the family gathering, to be completed when the members of the shattered household of earth shall be once more assembled.

Thus our brother's life was like the lives of us all—made up of sunshine and shadow.

And now he is also gone to that rest of which he often spoke in the sacred desk. As he sat desolate at the departure of the wife of his youth, so now another, the companion of his later years, sits bereaved and desolate at his departure. So the cup passes round the circle of human relationship.

Four children of our brother survive him. I remember them when they were young. I have heard of them as they passed out into the broad avenues of life. All reflect credit upon the home that reared them. All sit in the ashes of grief as they reflect upon the fact that they are now orphans. Surrounded they all are with the comforts, and even embellishments of life, but the presence of new friends, new relations, new surroundings, cannot shut out the home of their childhood, and close their ears to a father's prayers, their eyes to a mother's smiles and tears.

And now we bid our brother farewell "until the day-dawn and the shadows flee away."

But we shall not forget him. We shall think of him as still living, though absent. The inspiration of his love and life will abide with us. Heaven has now to us a new attraction. We shall not again hear his voice in the sacred desk, nor see him standing at the Lord's table, nor join with him in the sacred circle of the earthly home. We feel our loss. Could we impart to our brother the radiance and vigor of his youth, and reinstate him amid all the possibilities of the present, we might exert that power and say to him "Arise!" But even this would be involved in incongruities. The Lord gave, and the Lord has taken away. Our brother's work was done, and it was done well.

Still it is with us as it was with the disciples of our crucified Lord. They laid Him reluctantly away. Joseph of Arimathea with loving care laid upon the pulseless bosom the pierced hands, but he would far rather have clasped the hands of the living Christ. And so we lay our brother, Christ's minister, away. We place the evergreen upon his coffin. But O that sin had never begotten death, nor death a grave!

IV.

ADDRESS AT THE FUNERAL OF REV. WILLIAM T. SPROLE, D. D.,

AT THE FIRST PRESBYTERIAN CHURCH, DETROIT, JUNE 12, 1883, BY REV. GEO. D. BAKER, PASTOR.

I KNOW of nothing more beautiful, nothing which more glorifies the grace of God in sinful man, than a calm, peaceful, joyful and useful old age. Such an old age as was exemplified in him, God's loved and honored servant, whom today we are reverently carrying to his burial. He came among us when he was no longer young; at an age when ordinarily the buoyancy and sparkle of life have departed, and given place to a certain sedateness and gravity, indicative of the approach of the end. But how young we found him whom the years made old! How full of life and vigor, of cheer and hope! Into all our plans and projects how enthusiastically he entered as one "putting on" rather than "putting off the harness!" Instead of seeking rest and freedom from the burdens of the ministry, he coveted work —hard work. He insisted upon going to the front and hazarding his life "in the high places of the field." He was a veteran who had no desire for the retired list, but was ambitious for service where the battle was fierce and hot. We came to look upon him as a "minute man," ready at a moment's notice to go wherever he was called; and hence it was that he occupied a position among us, with reference to all our churches, the weaker as well as the stronger, which caused us to depend much upon him for counsel and for service. And he never once failed us, we never asked of him help in vain. Always loyal to our Church for Christ's sake, always true to us because we were Christ's servants, he was as a Bishop among us. There are man-made Bishops, and there are those constituted such by the Holy Ghost. God made him a Bishop, a man to command or to lead, and we willingly granted him his prerogative, "Primus inter pares." I desire to testify to-day, speaking for his brethren in the ministry, not only to his faithful and earnest service among us, but also to the generosity, the magnanimity, the unselfishness which ever and everywhere characterized it.

I have said that it was given us to know him only when the period of youth and middle age had passed, and he was drawing near the bound of life. But from what we saw and knew of him in these closing years, we can well believe all that is told us of his strength and beauty when he was in the midst of his days; that senators and judges at the capital of the nation hung upon his eloquent lips, while he instructed them in righteousness; that in the position to which he was called in the military school at West Point, he commanded the respect and even the affection of the students, as being himself a good soldier of Jesus Christ, while brimful of the loftiest and purest patriotism. But we envy not those who enjoyed his ministrations in those earlier years. We are content with what God gave us, his gentle, ripe, beneficent, blessed old age. We shall sadly, truly miss him, and often sigh for his strong and cheering presence. But, remembering his own example of hopefulness and courage, we will turn away from his bier to emulate his virtues, and, God helping us, to be "faithful unto death" even as was he. We are in sorrow but not in despair. When Frederic Barbarossa was leading his German Crusaders in the twelfth century on their march through Asia Minor to Jerusalem, he heard of the death of his only son. As the tears coursed down his snowy beard he turnèd to his army and said : "My son is dead, but Christ lives—Forward!" We mourn to-day the departure of our father, brother, friend, but we still hear those words which in dying he spake, illustrative of his faith and a reminder of the fulness of joys which now are his.

> "When I've been there ten thousand years,
> Bright shining as the sun,
> I've no less days to sing His praise,
> Than when I first begun."

We cannot, we do not think of him as dead. "He is alive for evermore." He has joined the blood-bought company of the elected and the chosen. He is in the presence of the King! God "has made him most blessed forever."

V.

THE LATE DR. SPROLE.

THE FUNERAL SERVICES—ADDRESS BY REV. DR. SUTHERLAND.

ADDITIONAL particulars contained in the following account of the funeral services taken from the *Indianapolis Journal* of June 14, 1883:

The funeral services of the late Rev. Dr. Sprole, who died at Detroit, Mich., Saturday, June 9, were held, on yesterday morning, at the residence of Mr. James Brown, according to notice. The remains arrived from Detroit on the morning train, in charge of Mr. D. M. Ferry, of Detroit, and were accompanied by his daughters, Mrs. Dunster, of Ann Arbor, and Mrs. Eastman, of Minneapolis, also his son, Prof. S. M. Sprole, from Brooklyn, N. Y. A large number of old settlers were present, to whom Dr. Sprole was well known in the early days of the city. The floral tributes were beautiful and profuse. The pail-bearers were ex-Governor Baker, John F. Wallick, John A. Holliday, Dr. C. N. Todd, Sergeant Wappenhaus, Thomas H. Sharpe and Dr. W. C. Thompson. The services were conducted by the Rev. Dr. Sutherland, of Jacksonville, Ill., assisted by Rev. Messrs. C. H. Raymond and L. G. Hay, of this city. Dr. Sutherland delivered the address, of which the following is a synopsis, as it appeared in the *Indianapolis Daily Journal:*

Were I simply to consult my own feelings upon this occasion, my humble tribute to the memory of him whose spirit has passed into the Unseen and Eternal would be that of silent grief. When the death angel summoned him to go hence, he summoned one of the most constant and devoted friends of my life. I have reason to believe that he watched my career with as much interest as if I had been his own son, and whatever success I have achieved in the vocation to which, in the providence of God, I have been called, the credit of it is in no small measure due to the wise counsel and kindly interest of our departed friend. His memory will ever be precious to me, and the thought that I held so warm a place in his affections will continue to be a source of unspeakable pleasure. In view of the friendship and affection which bound us together, you can appreciate, in some measure at least, my feelings upon this occasion. I only wish I were able to picture Dr. Sprole's life before you, to-day, in all the fulness, richness and beauty in which it lies in my own mind and heart. But the proprieties of the occasion demand that I should not speak of myself or for myself, but rather of the public life and labors of the deceased, and of these but briefly under the circumstances.

Born in the year 1809, his early life began almost with the beginning of our century, and continued throughout all these eventful years, growing in strength and beauty, in Christlikeness, to the close. As a man, Dr. Sprole was a prince among princes. He had doubtless his failings and weaknesses, but they were held in check by the higher self, which swayed the scepter of his princely manhood. In early life his associates were wisely chosen, and some of them, who subsequently became distinguished in the church and in the State, had much to do in the moulding of his character and the shaping of his future career—among whom might be mentioned the late Rev. Dr. Erskine Mason, of whose splendid talents and life-long friendship Dr. Sprole often spoke to myself when recalling the associates and recounting the experiences of other years. With such companionship our deceased friend entered upon his preparation for the Christian ministry, to which profession he had decided to consecrate his life and his talents. His literary studies were prosecuted in the College of Baltimore, and under the supervision of Rev. Dr. Duncan, who for upward of fifty years was the beloved pastor of the Fayette Street Church of that city. Dr. Sprole graduated from Princeton Seminary in the spring of 1830, and soon after his licensure came to this city, in company with his sister, Mrs. Colonel Blake, a lady in whose tender sympathies and widely known hospitality are manifested that family trait which so strikingly marked the character of her illustrious brother. Before returning East he spent several months in Terre Haute, and while there organized a Presbyterian church. On his return to Baltimore he received a call to become pastor of a Presbyterian church in Orange County, New York, and on his way to look over the field he remained a few days at Philadelphia with his friend, Mr. Chambers, and while there was waited upon by a committee from one of the German Reformed churches of the city, whose pastorate was then vacant. He was strongly urged by them to accept a call and become their pastor, which, after consulting his friends, he concluded to do. Although so young and inexperienced at the time, Dr. Sprole's pastorate in Philadelphia was marked by what might be truly called a phenomenal success. The membership increased within the three years of his ministry there, from about 50 to over 600. The success which attended his labors in Philadelphia brought him into widespread notice throughout the East, and when the Rev. Dr. Duffield resigned his charge of the First Presbyterian Church of Carlisle, Pa., he strongly urged his people to call Dr. Sprole, which they did. After some hesitation he accepted, and continued as pastor of that church for a period of about seven years, when he assumed the pastoral charge of the First Presbyterian Church of Washington, D. C., and was at the same time elected chaplain to Congress. The First Presbyterian Church was at the time known as the "Administration Church." President Polk and his family and a majority of the members of his cabinet were regular attendants there. Dr. Sprole's popularity in Washington was not won at the sacrifice of truth or by pandering to the whims and tastes of men. Like the great Apostle, he was ever determined not to know anything among the people save Jesus Christ and him crucified. In this connection it might not be out of place to relate an incident which strikingly illustrates Dr. Sprole's fidelity to the simple truth of the Cross, as well as the impression which his course in this regard made upon some of the leading men in Washington at the time of his pastorate there. The Unitarians had just organized a church and called a talented young man from Boston to become their pastor. A deputation from the new organization waited upon Rufus Choate, Senator from Massachusetts, and urged him to attend their services, believing, as they were free to say, that the distinguished Senator's presence would materially aid and popularize their new church venture. They said to Mr. Choate : " The gentleman whom we have called to the pastorate is a poet, a philosopher and an orator, and we have no doubt you would be charmed with his preaching." Senator Choate listened to them patiently until they got through, and then turning to the leader of the deputation firmly said : " I shall not attend your services, sir. When I want poetry I can go to the masters. When I want philosophy I can go to the original sources. When I want oratory I can do a little of it myself. But when I want to hear about the Lord Jesus Christ, I propose to go down to Four-and-a-half street to hear Mr. Sprole."

Toward the close of President Polk's term of office he appointed Dr. Sprole chaplain at West Point, which position he held for about ten years, when he was removed by President Pierce, at the instigation of the then Secretary of War, Jefferson Davis. The First Presbyterian Church of Newburgh, on the

Hudson, was vacant at the time, and Dr. Sprole was unanimously invited to become its pastor. This church had been weakened by dissensions and wrecked by divisions, but it was not long after Dr. Sprole assumed charge of it before harmony was restored and it began to show signs of new life and vigor, and when he resigned his charge, after a pastorate of about eighteen years, it was one of the largest, the most prosperous and most influential Presbyterian churches in this country. While settled at Newburgh, Dr. Sprole was twice called to his old charge in Philadelphia, as well as to several other prominent pulpits in the East. But these indications of popular favor, while they were doubtless gratifying to him, did not tend to make him restless in the position in which the providence of God had placed him. No man was ever freer from a self-seeking spirit than was he.

Whenever he spoke of his public career in my presence he never failed to make acknowledgements of God's goodness through it all; and in fact the same gratitude, the same spirit pervaded his references to his social and domestic relations. How often have I heard him use the expression, "O how thankful I ought to be to God for His great goodness toward me."

I shall not prolong this imperfect sketch of his life. After the resignation of his charge at Newburgh, his career is more or less familiar to all of you who are present here to-day. Almost to the close of his earthly life he continued to preach the gospel. It was his peculiar delight to tell "the old, old story of Jesus and His love." His preaching was always fresh, vigorous, scriptural and tender. He was one of those who in spirit never grow old. Although for four years living on "borrowed capital," as we say, he was, in the "inward man," which was renewed day by day, as youthful and buoyant as when he entered upon his first pastoral charge and charmed the multitudes by his fervid eloquence and persuasive appeals.

One of the chief excellencies and charms of his preaching was

his devotion to truth and the power of his own personality behind
his utterances. He himself lived the gospel he preached. This,
too, was largely the source of his personal influence over men.
When one stood in his presence he could not help feeling that he
was standing in the presence of a man worthy, to the fullest
extent, of his confidence and esteem ; one who ever strove to
exemplify the spirit and the teachings of his Master. It is a note-
worthy fact that never, during a public career of over half a
century, did he do aught that tended to bring reproach upon
himself or discredit upon the profession to which he belonged.
To all his noble qualities of mind and heart were added a com-
manding presence and grace of manner rarely to be met with.
Never would he permit himself to overstep the bounds of pro-
priety in his intercourse with men, or allow himself to disregard
the little courtesies which are due from man to his fellows, and
which throw a charm over social life. But why should I detain
you further ? To you, to the most of you at least, who are present
here to-day to pay your last tribute of respect to his memory, he
was known and appreciated. His life-work is ended. He has
gone to his rest and to his reward—a reward immeasurably great
in itself, and as I believe greater still in its possibilities. It but
remains for us to profit by the record of his noble and eventful
life, to imitate his virtues, and we too may look forward with confidence and expectancy to the time when we shall put off this our
clayey tabernacle and when our spirits shall be borne by the
angels to a new life,

> "Far from the discord loud,
> Far from the striving crowd,
> Far from the din,
> Far from the burning tears,
> Far from the trembling fears,
> Far from the sin."

CPSIA information can be obtained
at www.ICGtesting.com
Printed in the USA
BVHW060924041218
534639BV00018BA/919/P